# CONTENTS

# STEREOTYPICAL ESSEX GIRL AND BOY

Blonde or streaked blonde hair
Orange-coloured skin
Mobile phone
Vest top with bra showing
Celtic tattoo
Visible thong
Distressed denim mini-skirt
Big chunky belt
Ugg boots
Baby & pushchair as fashion accessory

Spiky gelled hair
Big mouth – often open for shouting
Chunky gold jewellery
Crop sleeved designer t-shirt
Traditional Celtic band tattoo
Bottle of whatever drink is trendy
Visible designer underpants
Distressed designer denim jeans
Ridiculously expensive designer trainers

# ·Essex·
# Sumfing Else!

## A Cornucopia of Estuary English

### Steve Crancher

**With illustrations by ASH
and by Richard Scollins**

COUNTRYSIDE BOOKS
NEWBURY BERKSHIRE

First published 2005
© Text – Steve Crancher, 2005
© Illustrations – Ashley Garrard, 2005

All rights reserved.
No reproduction permitted without the prior
permission of the publisher:

COUNTRYSIDE BOOKS
3 Catherine Road
Newbury, Berkshire

To view our complete range of books,
please visit us at
www.countrysidebooks.co.uk

ISBN 1 85306 950 7
EAN 978 1 85306 950 5

Both Publisher and Author acknowledge with
gratitude the debt they owe to *Ey Up Mi Duck!*
by Richard Scollins and John Titford, first published
in 1976. That book was the inspiration for this series.

Designed by Peter Davies, Nautilus Design
Produced through MRM Associates Ltd., Reading
Typeset by Techniset Typesetters, Newton-le-Willows
Printed by Woolnough Bookbinding Ltd., Irthlingborough

# INTRODUCTION

**E**ssex is a county in the very south-east corner of England, not including Kent and East Sussex. It's bigger than Luxembourg and, surprisingly, slightly bigger than some parts of Russia. Essex is bordered by London, Hertfordshire, Cambridgeshire (I think), Suffolk, the River Thames and the North Sea, which is rich in salt water. Our county has spawned many, many people over the years. Too many to mention.

The county town, Chelmsford, has been so (the county town I mean) for longer than even I can remember. And Colchester, in the north-east, is the oldest inhabited town in the whole of Great Britain. Now *that's* saying something.

Recently, the tomb of a Saxon king was unearthed in Prittlewell, near Southend. He is thought to have been buried there 1,000 years ago and, although his identity will never be known, experts can guess at his lifestyle as they marvel at their find. Nicknamed the 'King of Bling', he was, without doubt, an Essex man. Archaeologists discovered many artefacts, including chunky gold jewellery and an empty, faded bottle of hair dye. They also found a narrow, pointed object, some three inches in length. After much deliberation, it was concluded that this was the heel – and all that remained – of a stiletto-heeled shoe. Probably that of his wife, buried with him.

The dialect of Essex is complicated. The East Saxons probably had some sort of accent, now lost in the mists of time. Traditional Essex of today is akin to that of Suffolk, though with enough differences to make it distinctive. There is also a sub-dialect on the banks of the River Blackwater, used exclusively by fishermen there.

In the past 50 or 60 years, however, Londoners have ventured out into the county, bringing with them their own accent. The mixture has resulted in Estuary English, an accent that has become popular – fashionable, even – since the 1980s. Many traditionalists dislike the accent, describing it as common,

vulgar and lazy. There is, arguably, an element of truth in this but, nevertheless, Estuary English can now be heard throughout England. Yuppies of the 1980s embraced it, as did the BBC in its soap opera, *EastEnders*. Deregulation of the Stock Exchange saw the accent gradually replace Received Pronunciation there and, in a final act of acceptance, the Prime Minister famously glottal-stopped the letter T.

A glottal stop, incidentally, is where the letter T is not tapped, i.e. not pronounced distinctly. A speaker of Received Pronunciation, or BBC English, will tap the T distinctly, while a speaker of Estuary English will drop it, particularly when followed by another consonant. For example, the T in football would be replaced by a glottal stop, though when the T is followed by a vowel sound, e.g. Saturday, the T would probably be tapped.

The OU or OW sound is pronounced like a long, hard A. For example, 'It's your round,' becomes 'It's your raand.'

The letter H is usually dropped completely from the front of words. Head, hand and hip become ed, and and ip. This is, of course, in common with other accents throughout Britain.

TH is replaced by F at the beginning of a syllable, or a softer V elsewhere. Therefore, 'I fink,' and 'I ain't bovvered.'

The idea of this book is to take a sideways glance at Essex. It doesn't include Rochford's whispering court, in which trials were heard at midnight at the market town's King's Hill. Apparently, the lord of the manor returned home one night and overheard some locals speaking ill of him, in hushed voices. For some reason, now unknown, it inspired him to instigate the whispering court, and the tradition went on for many years.

Strange as it may seem, we won't bother ourselves with Thaxted's 'battle of the flags', when the socialist vicar hung the red flag in his church during the First World War. It was secretly removed, the vicar replaced it, it was removed and replaced again, until Rev Conrad Noel was told by the Church committee to get rid of it once and for all. At the time, it caused quite a sensation.

We will also fail to mention 'Cunning' James Murrell, from Hadleigh. Cunning, as his mates might have called him, was the seventh son of a seventh son, which probably put him in good stead for the reputation that was to come. He was supposed to have possessed supernatural powers, knew everything there was to know (like my mate, Dave) and could be in two places at the same time.

Boudicca will also get short shrift. She is included in passing but would have been more so had she not changed her name by deed poll, from Boadicea. And, anyway, she sacked Colchester, which was doing a pretty good job.

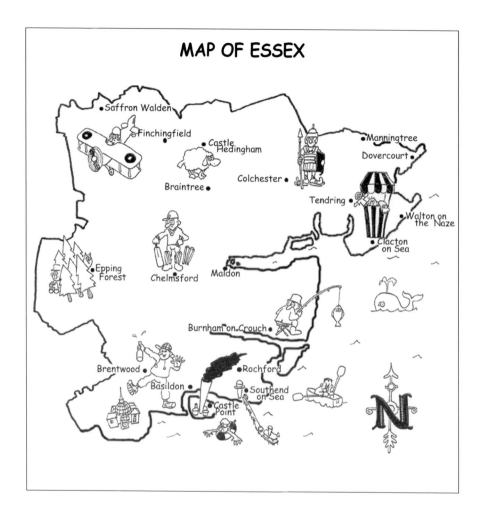

## MAP OF ESSEX

We will leave out altogether the 12th-century Dunmow Flitch. This was a trial of six married couples, who had been married at least a year and a day, to prove their faithfulness. The winning couple were awarded a flitch – or side – of bacon. The ceremony was reinstated in the 19th century and is still held every leap year.

The Witchfinder General, Matthew Hopkins, cannot be found in these pages. After all, he was a power-crazed man who persecuted womankind and pursued anyone accused of witchcraft. After starting his infamous career in his home town of Manningtree, he was responsible for many deaths throughout the region during the English Civil War.

However, although we have included the much-maligned Essex boy and Essex girl, we do so in the knowledge that such people are mere stereotypes. Essex has been used as an epithet for people that exist throughout Britain, and its continued use is, perhaps, unfair. But we also acknowledge that the Essex boy and Essex girl caricatures are found scattered as liberally across this county as any other – and so we happily take the *(insert capital P)* out of them.

Well, that's enough nattering from me. Let's get on with it, shall we?

(Someone said we ought to mention Harlow.)

*Steve Crancher*

DARREN WASN'T CONTENT WITH USING A 4 X 4,
LIKE EVERYONE ELSE, TO DRIVE HIS KIDS TO SCHOOL

# PLACES TO VISIT

There are as many as 27 places to visit in the whole of Britain, and almost half of these are in Essex. The county is famous for its mountain range, called the Malvern Hills, which runs north from Derbyshire as far as Hadrian's Wall, separating it from Suffolk in the north. We have chosen a well-researched selection of visitor attractions in Essex, starting with the most haunted place in the country:

## BORLEY RECTORY

Borley is a small village in the very north of the county, right beside the River Stour.

On 28th July, 1900, the ghost of a nun was seen by four people in the rectory garden. There were many more reports of inexplicable events and, 28 years later, the rector promptly wrote to the *Daily Mirror* asking for advice. (This action, perhaps, shows a degree of naivety and a distinct lack of taste.) Instead of advice, he got a journalist who wrote sensational articles about the haunting. After this, local coach firms organised 'Ghost Tours' and hundreds of people descended on the tiny village.

Despite the small detail of the rectory burning down in 1939, the attention has never ceased and frustrated locals removed road signs in a bid to deter unwanted visitors. As it's not there any more, though, it's not worth visiting.

## COLCHESTER

The oldest inhabited town in England. Colchester has a huge castle that's now a museum. Boudicca once lived here but she moved out when the army moved in. She was quoted in the local paper as saying: 'I ain't into soljas or urfquakes, so I fort I'd go somewhere a bit more quieter'. *(sic)*

# ESSEX – SUMFING ELSE!

THE KURSAAL, SOUTHEND-ON-SEA

## SOUTHEND-ON-SEA

Southend has a beach on the attractive Thames estuary. It also has a golden mile which is full of amusement arcades, pubs and cafes with exotic names, such as Dave's Donuts. There is an annual air show that attracts visitors from all over south Essex and, while they're there, the majority of the locals go out for the day. It has the longest pier in the world.

## CLACTON-ON-SEA

Clacton is like Southend but smaller. It used to have a Butlin's where everyone went at least once for a holiday. The redcoats now live in underground caves, feed on discarded apple peel, and practise dance routines.

## DEDHAM

'Iss a nice place, innit?' There's loads of old houses and a river with boats to hire. And you can get a cuppa there. This is called Constable country, because some pictures were painted here and hereabout.

## WALTON-ON-THE-NAZE

This is a seaside town where they go looking for fossils. Once, they found a 60-million-year-old gnat preserved in amber and, through the miracle of DNA, made a dinosaur which came alive and ate everybody. Walton-on-the-Naze also has the longest pier in Britain, not including Southend.

## FINCHINGFIELD

This has won prizes for being a pretty village. It has a big green in its centre with a river, a ford and a bridge. You can feed the locals here. I once saw a man with blond hair in a 4x4 going over the bridge. He didn't want to get his car wet.

## LEIGH-ON-SEA

Leigh is a suburb of Southend but with a sort of cobblestone-effect road. It's famous for its cockles, and overweight geezers stripped down to a pair of shorts and drinking pints of lager on hot, balmy evenings.

## HEDINGHAM CASTLE

The castle is actually a Norman keep, overlooking the attractive village called Castle Hedingham. I always get mixed up which is which – Hedingham Castle or Castle Hedingham.

### FRINTON-ON-SEA
Frinton doesn't really belong in Essex. For a seaside town, it's much too nice. They should move it up to Suffolk or somewhere.

### DOVERCOURT
*Hi-de-hi* was filmed here. Gladys Emmanuel Pugh still lives in Dovercourt. Su Pollard is banned because she just kept saying 'Hi-de-hi'.

### AUDLEY END
This is a glorious old stately home in Saffron Walden. It's a typically glorious old stately home with gardens and all that. I went there once when I was a kid and my mum wore a mini-skirt.

### BURNHAM-ON-CROUCH
Picture sunny days with yachts moored on a glistening, relaxing river, and blokes stripped down to their shorts, sitting outside picturesque pubs, drinking lager and swearing at the tops of their voices. That's Burnham-on-Crouch.

### EPPING FOREST
This is a big old place with lots of trees and stuff. About 100 years ago they decided to make the lakes bigger just so they could get the unemployment figures down. Henry the Eighth hunted here and bagged himself three squirrels, two wives and a sperm whale which had been attracted by the large lakes. Winston Churchill was the MP (before he died).

# ESSEX – SUMFING ELSE!

South Woodford

The Beach, Shoeburyness.

# TAKING THE WATERS

Only Cornwall has more coastline than Essex, and that's a long way away, so it doesn't matter. Water is therefore a dominant feature of life in our county, especially if you live near the beach, or maybe the swimming baths, or even if you have a paddling pool in your back garden.

The city of Bath was re-invented as a spa town in the 18th century after the Romans first discovered it hundreds of years before. As people flocked there, in the belief that the water was good for their health, so other spa towns began to appear. Royal Tunbridge Wells, Leamington and Harrogate are well-known examples, but there were many others – several of which were in Essex.

And then there is the yuppie's favourite drink – mineral water. Today, these products come from remote places, high up in the mountains somewhere. Their bottlers perpetuate images of clear streams trickling through cool rocks, straight over a waterfall where some bloke is standing, holding a bottle with the lid off, and waiting for it to reach 500 millilitres. Towns like Buxton, Malvern and Sparkling Perrier sound ideal to put on the label. But would they sell so well if they were named after Tilbury or Vange? Here are a few of those that have come and gone in Essex.

## TILBURY

A farmer named Kellaway sank a well at Tilbury in 1724 and soon became aware of its medicinal properties. It alleviated symptoms of colds, gout and diarrhoea when he drank it and he recommended it to his farm workers.

It sounds undrinkable by today's standards – the water was described as being the colour of light straw and tasting like milk. Mr Kellaway's farm workers must have taken a mouthful, nodded enthusiastically, then spat it out when he wasn't looking. And after this, no doubt, they kept it quiet when they were feeling under the weather.

Despite that, it was given to friends in London, and a little later, Dr John Andree was using it to treat his patients. Then it was put on sale at one shilling (5 pence) a bottle.

In 1779 John Ellison took over the well, by which time the product was called Tilbury Alterative Water, and it was now being sold all over the country. For a few years, Tilbury water was a fashionable drink.

However, a competitor sank a new well close to the previous one. It was advertised vigorously and bottled with a seal so as to make it seem like the genuine article. Mr Ellison countered with a scientific report on the medicinal qualities of his original water. But the two of them began to lose business as sea water was now becoming fashionable and, by 1800, both had lost their popularity.

## VANGE

Another surprising contender in the mineral water market was Vange, these days a suburb of Basildon. However, in 1922, it was a national sensation, and the public clamoured for Vange Water.

In 1898, the farmer at Hovells Farm dug a well, didn't like the taste of the water, and so gave it to his cattle. The cows loved it, though, and thrived. News of this spread to London and Edwin Cash, the owner of the Angel Hotel, in Islington, after having it analysed, hurried down to Vange and promptly bought part of the farm.

Twenty years later he decided to do something about it. He set up a limited company, dug a second well and started bottling and selling the water.

Then, in 1922, the *Westminster Gazette* ran a story about an 80-year-old who used the water to make tea and was feeling like a new man. Suddenly, people flocked to Vange and queues quickly built up. Business was so good that Mr Cash had to start limiting the amounts sold and one day his company was unable to cope with demand. They put up a notice stating the water had been sold for the day. Someone told the *Westminster Gazette* about this, and they reported that the wells had dried up. Mr Cash sued the paper for libel and settled out of court.

Now, a rival firm was set up on a nearby farm and the two went head to head, with advertised claim and counter claim. However, it all went wrong when a sanitary inspector reported the water was unfit for domestic consumption, as it contained organic material. Within two years, both businesses had closed.

## HOCKLEY

Mr Fawcett slapped Mr Reed on the back and called him a jolly good fellow. Mr Reed reciprocated. Mr Mayne joined the mutual backslapping, and the three

worthy gentlemen – proprietors – toasted the Queen before hooking their thumbs into their lapels and delivering speeches and platitudes to everyone present.

It was June 1843, and those gathered were happily rubbing their hands with glee, anticipating the money rolling in, now that Hockley Spa had opened for business.

Several years earlier, a Mrs Clay had moved with her husband to Hockley and began to drink the water. Before long, her asthma improved, word got about and people started visiting the village for their health.

The place was developed as a health resort and, along with the spa room, a hotel was built to attract visitors. The ostentatiously-furnished spa room took a year to build.

However, there was no railway station in Hockley at this time. A few people did arrive but, apart from taking in the water, there was nothing for them to do. They were bored silly. And so the grand venture failed almost as soon as it had begun.

Several attempts have been made over the years to resurrect Hockley Spa, but all have fallen by the wayside. The building still survives though, waiting for its next big adventure.

## WITHAM

The success of Witham Spa seems to have been down to the effort and enterprise of one man, who seems to have been Dr James Taverner.

The spa had originally been discovered in the 1600s but in the 1730s Dr Taverner saw the financial possibilities, particularly because of the town's location on the Essex Great Road, which ran from London to Norwich, and back again.

Taverner made a long list of the ailments, disorders and maladies that were cured by Witham's mineral water and went on to say it was volatile and didn't travel well. An assembly room was built to host dancing, the place was fervently advertised to ladies and gentlemen of 'a genteel appearance and nature', and Witham became a fashionable spa town.

The Assembly Room was said to have been built from a section of New Hall at nearby Boreham, as two wings were demolished at the time.

Sadly, in 1746, Dr Taverner died and the glory days of Witham Spa died with him. The spa continued until the end of the 18th century, when, as at Tilbury, sea bathing became fashionable.

Taverner had said the water was 'attenuating, resolving, dessicative, balsamick, pectoral, vulnerary and antiscobutick'.

Nuff said!

## DOVERCOURT

So, Witham lost out to sea bathing, and Hockley to its isolated location. But Dovercourt was well placed for both and, consequently, had the longest lifespan of all Essex spas.

The timing was perfect. It commenced trading in 1854, on precisely the same day in August as the railway to Harwich was opened. And it was right beside the sea, so visitors could alternate between fresh spring water and sea water.

The man behind the venture was Harwich MP, John Bagshaw. In the grounds of his cliff-top home, he rediscovered the spring – once used by the Romans – and promptly built two hotels and a spa complex, incorporating a pump room, a reading room and a reception.

Advice was given that visitors should drink the water first thing in the morning, while taking gentle exercise. They were then pointed in the direction of the boating facilities and the garden walks. Business was thriving.

However, Bagshaw's interest waned and he sold it on. The spa continued to attract visitors but, by 1910, it had fallen into disuse. Royal Engineers were billeted there during the First World War and, although there were ongoing talks to revive the spa in 1920, the whole kit and caboodle was knocked down.

Clacton

# HERO & VILLAIN

**M**any well-known people have originated in Essex and included in their number is one of the most heroic and also one of the most infamous in British history.

**Dick Turpin** is remembered in legend as a gentleman highwayman, who rode his trusty steed, Black Bess, non-stop to York in a matter of hours – galloping headlong and leaping over turnstiles – in order to establish an alibi. The handsome scoundrel always removed his tricorn hat when in the company of ladies, and never failed to treat his victims with the utmost courtesy.

Sadly, this image was created by author Harrison Ainsworth in his novel, *Rockwood*, which was published in 1834 – almost 100 years after Turpin was hanged.

In reality, Dick Turpin was described as having a pock-marked face. He was a farmer's son, born at Hempstead, a small village in the north of Essex, in 1705. Apprenticed to a butcher, Turpin went into business in Waltham Abbey, where he married an innkeeper's daughter called Hester Palmer.

After a bout of cattle stealing, he headed for the coast and robbed smugglers, purporting to be a revenue officer. But he was soon on the run again – this time to Epping Forest, where he joined Gregory's Gang, notorious for their poaching and burgling activities. During one of these burglaries, he is said to have sadistically held a woman over a fire until she revealed the whereabouts of the valuables.

When three members of Gregory's Gang were caught and hanged, Turpin and his partner-in-crime, Rowden, took to highway robbery and, in 1735, were active in the north London area. Later he paired up with Tom King and the two became notorious, particularly in and around Epping. In 1737, Turpin murdered Thomas Morris, who was trying to apprehend him, at Fairmead Bottom, near Chingford. Shortly after this, he accidentally shot and killed his friend, Tom King.

There was a huge bounty on his head so Turpin decided to move up to Long Sutton in Lincolnshire. However, unable to stay out of trouble, he moved north again, this time to York. Here, he changed his name to John Palmer but was finally caught, and his true identity revealed, when he wrote a letter to his brother in Essex, asking for help. His ex-schoolmaster recognised his handwriting and reported it. Turpin went to the gallows in 1739, aged 34. A mere pup, as far as I'm concerned.

**Lawrence Edward Grace Oates** is remembered for his heroic sacrifice during the ill-fated expedition to the South Pole in 1912. Knowing that his frostbitten limbs rendered him a hindrance and a drain on the team's resources, he hoped he would die overnight in a frozen tent. When he woke up the next morning, it was blowing a blizzard. Oates said, 'I am just going out. I may be some time.' He was never seen again.

Lawrence was born in Putney, London, in 1880. As a child, he was constantly sick. But his family moved to the village of Gestingthorpe, a short distance from the Suffolk border. The house was Gestingthorpe Hall, also known as Over Hall. He grew to love horses and, when he was occasionally sent to South Africa by his parents in the hope the experience would improve his health, he was always keen to get home to his horses.

The teenage Lawrence was a strong man. At 18 years old, he got a commission in a cavalry regiment, and at 20 he was sent to the Boer War. His brave actions here earned him the nickname 'No Surrender Oates', but they also earned him a bullet wound in the thigh, which gave him a limp for the rest of his life.

On his return to Gestingthorpe, his mother celebrated by paying for the restoration of the church bells. Two of the bells are still inscribed in his honour.

After serving out his time in the army, Lawrence took to hunting. But when he heard the news that Captain Scott was putting together a team to be the first to the South Pole, he jumped at the chance to join, offering his expertise with both dogs and horses. The expedition became a race between the British team and Roald Amundsen's Norwegian team.

Scott and his team reached the South Pole on 17th January, 1912, but found the Norwegians had got there before them. On the journey back, the weary, weakened party faced exceptionally cold weather and, sadly, none of them survived the ordeal.

The church in Gestingthorpe, just across the road from the hall, now has a plaque on the wall. On it is inscribed:

> A very gallant gentleman Lawrence Edward Grace Oates, captain in the Inniskilling Dragoons. Born March 17 1880. Died March 17 1912, on the return journey from the South Pole of the Scott Antarctic expedition – when all were beset by hardship, he being gravely injured went out into the blizzard to die in the hope that by so doing he might enable his comrades to reach safety. This tablet is placed here in affectionate remembrance by his brother officers, AD 1913.

# WHO ATE ALL THE PIES?

**E**dward Bright was born in Maldon on 1st March, 1721. In his lifetime, he was known as the 'largest man that ever lived in this Island'.

By the age of twelve, he weighed ten stone, but nine years later this had increased to over 24 stone.

In his youth, Edward rode to Chelmsford every day in his job as a post-boy. Each day he drank a gallon of beer, plus half a pint of wine but, later, when he was told to cut down, he reduced his intake to four pints.

Eventually, there wasn't a horse in the land that could take Edward's weight, so he became a candlemaker and a grocer. When Big Ted visited London, he attracted attention, becoming a 'gazing stock and admiration of all people'. Pictures of him were printed and sold throughout Europe. A caption read: 'His legs were as big as a middling man's body'.

He was regularly bled by doctors, sometimes taking as much as two pints, but his health was a constant problem.

When he died in 1750, Edward weighed 44 stone, six pounds. He was five feet, nine-and-a-half inches tall, with a chest measurement of 66 inches and an 83-inch waist. His inside leg was never measured, as no one could get a tape measure to the top. He left a widow and five children, and his wife was pregnant with a sixth at his death.

His coffin was six feet, seven inches long and three feet deep. In order to get it out of the house, a hole was cut in the bedroom floor through which to lower it and the front door space was widened.

Just before his death, Edward had sent his waistcoat to a tailor to be let out. This waistcoat became the subject of a bet between a Mr Codd and a Mr Hance, that five men could fit into it. Not only five, but seven men got into the jacket.

Edward, though, was described as a very honest tradesman, a facetious companion, comely in his person, affable in his temper, a tender father and valuable friend.

Edward Bright, the fat man of Maldon, now has a street and a beer named after him.

In 1790, Edward's son, also named Edward, died aged 45. He was recorded as being about half the weight of his father. He left nine children.

| | |
|---|---|
| **a cutla** | two 'Me and Shaz 'av got a cutla kids' |
| **a cutla quid** | a small, unspecified amount of money 'Lend us a cutla quid, wilya, Dave?' 'Yeh. 'Ow much ja want?' 'A fiver' |
| **a mustard mitt** | preface to speaking frankly and honestly 'A mustard mitt, I d'narf fancy Sharon' |
| **all saffisticated** | educated, refined, cultured |
| **am samwij** | snack comprising two slices of bread with a piece of pig meat between, often served with mustard or pickle – luvverly |
| **an'all** | also |
| **andalwit** | cope 'Thass the job. Ja fink ya can andalwit?' |
| **anky panky** | naughtiness |
| **annual** | consequently 'You keep doing that annual get a clump ran the ear' |
| **arf panda** | a very big hamburger |
| **arst** | past tense of 'ask' |
| **art set** | covet 'He ad iz art set on that Gameboy' |
| **ass wicked man** | that's very good; I approve |
| **aya** | how are you; hello |
| **backander** | a secret payment, usually delivered in an unmarked, brown envelope |
| **bang aat of order** | behaving in a manner contrary to one's peers |
| **bettern'I** | I ought (literal translation: better hadn't I) |
| **big time** | plentifully 'It all wennoff big time' |
| **big wedge** | a healthy bank balance see also: wedge |

**bin**  past participle of 'to be' *'Where the ell av you bin till this time o' night?'*

**bort**  purchased

**brew**  cup of tea

**car near ya**  please speak up

**chav**  working class youth who wears a baseball cap, a hoodie, jogging bottoms and trainers. Chavs like to pretend they're tough, by swearing.

**chizalot**  thank you very much

**chuffed**  happy; proud

**chuffed to bits**  very happy

**clove**  to put on clothes

**cloze**  garments worn on the body

A PACK OF LESSER SPOTTED CHAVS
SURVEY THEIR PREY

**cort a panda**  a big hamburger, though not as big as an *arf panda*

**crack (one) up**  amuse

**d'narf**  very much *'Ere Sharon, I d'narf love you'*

**dan in the maff**  unhappy; depressed

**dane age**  in modern/present times *'You doan often see that, not in this dane age'*

**dijja**  did you *'So, dijja like ya dinner?'*

**dint**  did not *'Nuh, I dint'*

**dintya**  did you not *'Why dintya like ya dinner?'*

**do wot?**  I beg your pardon?

**doan**  do not *'Coz I doan like Brussels sprats'*

**doancha**  do you not *'Doancha like carrots?'*

**doddle**  simple task

**done rubbish**  performed badly *'West Am done rubbish this season'*

**donut**  idiot

**drekkun?**  do you consider?

**dunnit**  doesn't it *'Looks like it's gonna rain, dunnit'*

**earake**  an excuse for telling someone to quieten down *'Givvit a rest, wilya? Ya givvin me earake'*

| | |
|---|---|
| **earbashin** | to talk incessantly *'Ere look. She's givvin im a right old earbashin'* |
| **earner** | money-making scheme *'Thass a nice little earner'* |
| **eeva** | one or the other |
| **eeyar** | there you are (when giving) |
| **eez** | 1. he is; 2. belonging to him |
| **elf** | the state of being fit and well |
| **erz** | belonging to her |
| **eyebrow** | intellectual; cultured |
| **fearta** | a building used for dramatic performance |
| **feery** | speculative thought *'My feery is it's run aat of petrol'* |
| **fink** | ponder |
| **for cryin aat laad** | mild expletive showing annoyance or surprise |
| **fort** | past tense of fink |
| **fortful** | meditative |
| **fortless** | careless of consequences or others' feelings |
| **frages** | recently *'I ain't done that frages'* |
| **freak me aat** | worry me |
| **frilla** | an exciting film |
| **frooan froo** | thoroughly; completely *'I'm an Essex gell frooan froo'* |
| **furralee** | thoroughly |
| **Furrock** | the area where Lakeside is. Also incorporates the towns of Graze, Stanford-no-Hope, Corrinam, Tilbry and Chavwell St Mary, not to mention Chavford Hundred |
| **gander** | look *(note on usage: Gander is used as a noun, not as a verb. One would not say 'Ere Dave, gander at that'. The correct use is 'Ere Dave, avva gander at that'.)* |
| **get ere** | come hither *(command to dog or child, as in 'Oi! Get ere!')* |
| **givvit a rest** | a request to discontinue speech or action, often used with the suffix *'wilya'* |

| | |
|---|---|
| **gobsmacked** | flabbergasted |
| **guess wot** | unanswerable and rhetorical question often used as a prelude to the announcement of news *'Guess wot? Dave's bort izself a new motah'* |
| **gutted** | upset; disappointed |
| **I aineeva** | neither have/am I |
| **innee** | is he not; has he not *'Dave's gone and got izself a job, innee'* |
| **innit** | 1. is it not; 2. *superfluous suffix: 'I'm goan daan the tansenter, innit'* |
| **intshee** | is she not |
| **intya** | are you not |
| **iss anart, innit** | that's very clever |
| **iz** | belonging to him |
| **izself** | himself |
| **ja?** | do you?; did you? |
| **jafta?** | is it really necessary? *(shows mild annoyance)* |
| **jamember?** | do you remember? |
| **janartamean?** | do you know what I mean? *See also nartamean?* |
| **janoe?** | do you know? |
| **juicy?** | did you see? *'Juicy Fools 'n' awsses lars night?'* |
| **just the job** | perfect; ideal; spot on |
| **laters** | goodbye for now |
| **leave it** | desist in action or speech |
| **leave it aat** | expression of disagreement |
| **leggit** | run away |
| **less** | let us *'Ere, less go daan the pub'* |
| **lessalook** | please can I see? |
| **me** | my *'She's me bird'* |
| **moody** | poor quality |
| **mug** | naïve person |
| **muppet** | idiot |
| **nartamean?** | do you know what I mean? *See also janartamean?* |
| **nasty niff** | offensive odour |

| | |
|---|---|
| **naya** | now; this very moment *'Get ere naya!'* |
| **nayaint** | no, I haven't |
| **neeva** | not one nor the other |
| **never** | did not *'You said you woz gonna elp'* *'No I never'* |
| **NHS** | National Elf Service |
| **nice one** | congratulations; well done |
| **no wurriz** | 1. never mind; 2. you're welcome |
| **o maiden** | a cake, pie, etc, made from basic ingredients in the kitchen, usually by someone's auntie *'Wanna bit of apple pie? It's an o maiden'* |
| **oi** | excuse me |
| **oi oi** | hello – Traditional male greeting in a pub |
| **ooja** | who do you *'Ooja fink'll win the cup?'* |
| **oppit** | go away |
| **out** | out of order *'you're well out'* |
| **pacific** | specific |
| **pain** | nuisance |
| **pants** | nonsense; disagreeable |
| **propaganda** | a good look |
| **proper** | extremely *'That woz proper good'* |
| **pukka** | very good; agreeable |
| **put a kettlon** | boil water in preparation for a cup of tea |
| **quality** | good |
| **raging ump** | extremely angry |
| **randeer** | locally |
| **razz** | arguments *'We bin avvin a lot of razz lately'* |
| **result** | favourable outcome, victory *'Nelson got a result at Trafalgar'* |
| **right ake** | well upset |
| **sad** | unfashionable; stupid |
| **shut it** | be quiet |
| **shwee** | shall we |

| | |
|---|---|
| **slater** | goodbye for now |
| **slootly** | absolutely |
| **snot** | it is not |
| **sot init** | it's unusually warm today |
| **spoze** | be inclined to think *'I spoze you wanna go daan the pub then'* |
| **stifficut** | certificate |
| **stuns** | plenty *'Stuns of chavs rand ere'* |
| **sumfing** | an unspecified, unknown thing |
| **sumfing else!** | exceptional! |
| **suvven** | from the south |
| **sweet azza nut** | splendid |
| **take ome** | net wage |
| **thass** | that is |
| **thez** | there is; there are |
| **too-free** | several *'How much wedge ya got on ya?' 'Abat too-free pans'* |
| **ump** | upset; angry — usually, *the ump* |
| **view erd?** | introductory phrase *'View erd? Craig's getting itched'* |
| **wawazat?** | I beg you're pardon? |
| **webbats** | in which place, specifically *'Webbats ja live?'* |
| **wejja** | where did you |
| **wellot** | extremely spicy *'This curry's wellot'* |
| **wernit** | was it not |
| **wez** | where is; where are |
| **wicked** | cool; very good |
| **wid** | we had; we should *'Wid better get going'* |
| **wilya** | will you |
| **wojja** | what do you *'Wojja want?'* |
| **wossatallabout?** | I don't understand |
| **wot you on?** | you are acting/talking in an unusual manner |
| **yad** | you had *'Yad to look, dintya'* |
| **yafta** | you must, you are obliged |
| **yooz lot** | everyone present |

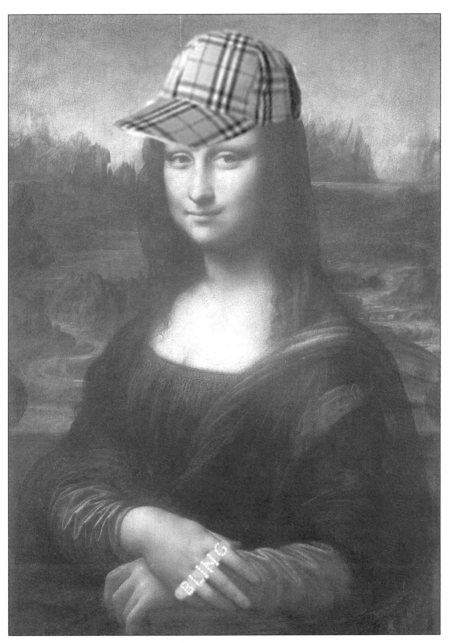

Essex Maid with Rings, *Leonardo da Canvey*. Early 16th century

E ssex has always led the way with pretty much everything. Baseball caps with the initials NY on them were invented in Basildon. Guglielmo Marconi was pretty much an Essex man when he sorted out radio signals. And Rayleigh High Street was the planned location for the filming of *Lord Of The Rings*, until director Peter Jackson took a holiday in New Zealand and decided it was slightly better.

But in 1016, a full 50 years before King Harold (the Vincible?) copped it at Hastings, Essex had its very own battle – at Ashingdon.

Danish king Canute (whose famous command to the tide is rumoured to have happened at Westcliff-on-Sea, just up from the Rossi's kiosk) had been doing a bit of plundering and was making his way back to the River Crouch, where his ships were anchored. (He wasn't on his own, by the way; he was with a load of his men.)

Anyway, Edmund Ironside – son of Ethelred and Elgiva (not Emma, also known as Aelfgifu, who was the daughter of Richard, Duke of Normandy, Ethelred's second wife and the mother of Alfred and Edward, but not Athelstan and Eadwig (not to be confused with Eadric) whose mother was indeed the aforementioned Elgiva – at least, I think that's right). Where was I? Oh yes, Edmund Ironside, who was the Saxon king at the time, had been following Canute. He caught up with him at Ashingdon. (Edmund Ironside wasn't on his own either, by the way; he also had a load of men with him.) As always with these kings, there was a bit of nepotism going on – he had his brother-in-law Eadric in charge of a load of other men.

Canute was at Canewdon, Edmund at Ashingdon and, after a bit of pushing and shoving, they had a big fight on the land between. The Saxons were having the best of it when the scheming Eadric decided that Canute looked the better bet. So Eadric pretended he had a bit of a stomach ache and he – and his men – legged it. That left Edmund up the creek and Canute won the day.

Going back to AD 893, there was another bit of a ding-dong, at Benfleet.

The Danes had sailed up the Thames hoping to do a bit of damage and cause some general mayhem. But things didn't go as planned so they put their boats in reverse and ended up at Benfleet where one of them, Haestan, had a fort.

They were planning to stay there for a bit because they were well knackered from all the fighting they'd been doing. But the Saxons had other plans. They came down from London and charged down the hills from Hadleigh and Thundersley.

It was all over in a flash, really. The Saxons killed the Danes, burnt their boats and took their women and nippers back to London, where King Alfred gave them a wink and said, 'Go on, on yer way. And don't do it again!' And Haestan, at least, was grateful to him and didn't.

A few Danes escaped from Benfleet and got themselves across to Shoebury. But they didn't like it much, except maybe East Beach, where they had a barbecue before taking a well-earned nap, and getting a ferry or something back to mainland Europe.

\* \* \*

The Battle of Maldon, in AD 991, is remembered in an epic Anglo Saxon poem, although most of us forget it – especially the verses.

What happened is this: The Vikings sailed up the River Blackwater and landed at Northey Island. The idea was to charge across the causeway that linked the island with Maldon at low tide. But the Saxon leader, Birhtnoth (and his men) were waiting for them and, anyway, the tide was in.

So the Vikings (who were probably wearing those big, horned helmets, like Tony Curtis and Kirk Douglas in the film of the same name) sent a few of their men over the causeway, but it was no good. They tried it a few times and lost a few soldiers in the process.

Instead, they resorted to Plan B – shouting across, 'You Saxons, you have big ears', 'Your mothers smell of jam,' and 'You can't fight for toffee' and stuff like that.

The Saxons were getting well wound up with this tactic of verbal abuse, which gave the Vikings a good chuckle. After a while, the Vikings said 'Come on then. Let's come over there and have a fair fight! Or are you chicken or something?'

Birhtnoth, who was fed up with always having to spell his name, ('No, not Birthnoth – Birhtnoth! The H is silent!') wasn't having any of that.

'Yeh, come on then,' he said. 'I'll show you who's chicken, you big yellas!'

(By 'yellas' he meant both 'people with yellow streaks up their backs' and 'people who shout too much' which he thought was right clever.)

So the Vikings strolled across the causeway, everyone had a fair fight, and Birhtnoth and his men were all killed.

\* \* \*

In 1379, Richard II's advisers decided it was a good idea to bring in a poll tax of one groat per person. This was grudgingly accepted. But two years later, Parliament increased it to three groats and the people of England were as happy with this as they would have been with, say, sticking pineapples up their noses.

In Essex, the people of Fobbing, Corringham and Stanford-le-Hope in particular were well upset.

'We ain't paying it,' they said, folding their arms indignantly.

A couple of top blokes were sent down, at different times, from London to Brentwood to try to sort it all out, but the men were having none of it and sent them packing with fleas in their ears. The second time, they got a bit carried away and killed some of the top bloke's cronies.

Now they marched up to London where they met up with all the revolting peasants from Kent, who were led by Wat Tyler. There were about 30,000 of them by this time.

King Richard, who was only 14 years old, agreed to meet the guys for a chat. What Tyler stepped forward but he was being disrespectful and, eventually, Richard told one of his goons to arrest him. Anyway, it all gets a bit complicated here but Wot Tyler, an archbishop and a chancellor all got killed. A handful of people stuck a few heads on poles but the majority decided it wasn't worth having your head stuck on a pole just to save three groats, so they traipsed off home.

However, about 500 men went to Norsey Wood in Billericay, but the army followed them in and killed them. And that was the end of that.

\* \* \*

During the English Civil War, there was a siege at Colchester. It was in 1648 when some Cavaliers went into the town – it was walled at the time – and waited for reinforcements.

The Roundheads camped outside, phoned for pizzas and sent their privates out for fish, chips and a gherkin (the Roundheads were known to be quite partial to gherkins). Meanwhile, within the walls, the hungry Cavaliers had to start eating dogs and horses. After two months, they ran out of dogs and horses and gave up. Their leaders were taken to the castle and shot.

There's a monument in the grounds marking the spot. An ancient legend says that the grass will never grow there, so the council tarmacked it, just to make sure. Go and have a gander. Go on.

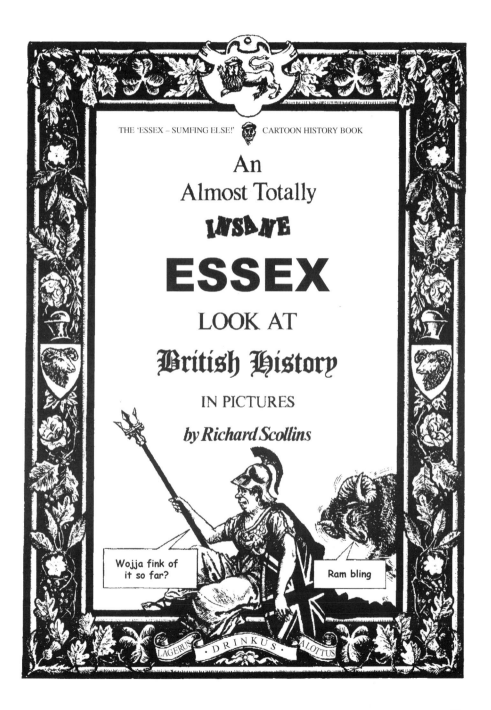

THE 'ESSEX – SUMFING ELSE!' CARTOON HISTORY BOOK

# An Almost Totally

# INSANE

# ESSEX

## LOOK AT

# British History

### IN PICTURES

*by Richard Scollins*

Wojja fink of it so far?

Ram bling

LAGERUS · DRINKUS · ALOTTUS

**Alfred and the Cakes — AD 878**

## Canute Demonstrates His Inability to Turn the Tide — AD 1020

## Lady Godiva — AD 1057

**The Battle of Hastings — AD 1066**

## The Death of William Rufus — AD 1100

**King John and Magna Carta — 1215**

**Edward I Presents His Son as
Prince of Wales — 1284**

**The Battle of Agincourt — 1415**

**Richard III at Bosworth — 1485**

**Henry VIII and Anne Boleyn — 1529**

**Francis Drake Goes Bowling — 1588**

## The Gunpowder Plot — 1605

**The Execution of Charles I — 1649**

**Bonnie Prince Charlie Arrives
in Scotland — 1745**

## Nelson at Trafalgar — 1805

## Wellington Inspects His Troops — 1815

**Stanley Greets Dr. Livingstone — 1871**

**Queen Victoria 'Not Amused' — 1878**

SAFF'END